Richard T. Ely

Pullman

A Social Study

Richard T. Ely

Pullman
A Social Study

ISBN/EAN: 9783337417857

Printed in Europe, USA, Canada, Australia, Japan

Cover: Foto ©Suzi / pixelio.de

More available books at **www.hansebooks.com**

Nº 417-FEBRUARY-1885 = ONE SHILLING

HARPER'S MONTHLY MAGAZINE

SAMPSON LOW, MARSTON, SEARLE AND RIVINGTON
188. FLEET STREET.————————LONDON—E·C

VOLUME 70.
NUMBER 417. } HARPER'S MAGAZINE. { LONDON,
FEBRUARY, 1885.

CONTENTS.

LONDON: SAMPSON LOW, MARSTON, SEARLE AND RIVINGTON,
CROWN BUILDINGS, 188, FLEET STREET, E.C.

THE ARCADE AND PUBLIC SQUARE.

PULLMAN: A SOCIAL STUDY.

COMMUNISM, socialism, nihilism, are international words. Understood by people of both hemispheres and of many tongues, and printed daily in ten thousand journals, they are evidence of a momentous social movement. They mean far more than the creeds which under these names find a comparatively limited acceptance. They bear witness to a widespread discontent with things as they are in modern society—a discontent which but rarely goes to the extreme length of what is ordinarily designated by the generic term socialism. The pretty dream of a perfect, natural order of things brought about by the free play of unrestrained social forces has vanished. It has given place on the one hand to pessimism; on the other, and more generally, to a determination not to let things go on of themselves, but to make them go in such manner as may be desired. The conviction has become general that the divine order never contemplated a social and economic world left to itself. Material is furnished out of which man must construct a social fabric according to his lights. This is what modern socialism means, and for this reason it is practical, not romantic, and leaving the dim, artificial light of the study, goes forth into the broad sunlight, seeking immediate realization among the people. This is what co-operation means. It is looked upon as a new social form. For this reason it is preached as a gospel, and its spread in England heralded with joy by men like Thomas Hughes. Finally, for brevity's sake, passing over numerous manifestations of this spirit in our times, this is what is meant by the many attempts of "captains of industry" to step in between those they lead and the unrestrained action of existing economic forces. The variety of methods to which recourse is had is great. Insurance of one kind and another, gratuitous instruction, amusements, reading-rooms, participation in profits, rewards for special merit, occur at once to the mind. Several employers have attempted more far-reaching establishments which should embrace the home life of laborers, and thus include wives and children in their beneficence. Interesting examples are the "Social Palace" of M. Godin at Guise, France, and the town of Saltaire, founded by Sir Titus Salt, on the banks of the Aire, in England, both of which have been described in the pages of this Magazine. Another instance is afforded by the works of the Willimantic Company, at Willimantic, Connecticut. But the most extensive experiment of this character is that now in progress at Pullman, Illinois. It is social experimentation on a vast scale, and this is its significance.

For this reason it challenges attention and discussion at a time when dynamite bombs and revolutionary murmurings terrify monarchs, when an enlarged human sympathy encircles the earth with beneficent institutions, and when an eager interest in social and economic facts more than atones for general indifference to the dogmatic assumptions of classic political economy.

Pullman, a town of eight thousand inhabitants, some ten miles from Chicago, on the Illinois Central Railroad, was founded less than four years ago by the Pullman Palace Car Company, whose president and leading spirit is Mr. George M. Pullman. Its purpose was to provide both a centre of industry and homes for the employés of the company and such additional laborers as might be attracted to the place by other opportunities to labor. Simply as a town, Pullman has not sufficient interest to justify a description of it in a great magazine. Its natural beauties are not remarkable, situated as it is on the low prairie land surrounding Chicago, and its newness makes such romances impossible as one can associate with villages like Lenox, and Stockbridge, and other ancient towns in New England. Like many other Western cities, its growth has been rapid, its population having increased from four souls in January, 1881, to 2084 in February, 1882, and to 8203 in September, 1884. A manufacturing town, it embraces the principal works of the Pullman Palace Car Company, in addition to the Allen Paper Car-wheel Company, the Union Foundry and Pullman Car-wheel Company, the Chicago Steelworks, the Steel-forging Company, and numerous less important enterprises.

Many of the last-mentioned are connected with building operations in the town of Pullman, or furnish commodities to its residents, and in many cases they also supply customers elsewhere, such as the gasworks, the ice-houses, the brick-yards,

A STREET IN PULLMAN.

the carpenter shops, and the large farm which receives the sewage of Pullman. The number of men employed in the place is at present about four thousand, of whom over three thousand are employed by the Palace Car Company. The products of the various establishments are valued at many millions of dollars. As all the Pullman enterprises are conduct-

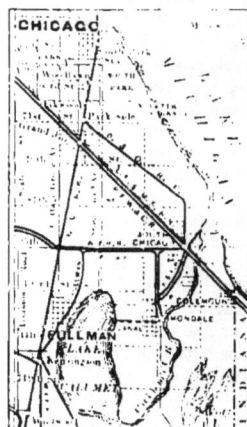

SUBURBS OF CHICAGO.

THE MARKET-HOUSE.

ed with what seems to the writer a needless air of secrecy, reliable statistics are obtained with difficulty. However, the car-works claim a capacity to turn out $8,000,000 worth of passenger and freight cars per annum, and it is expected that they will be able to manufacture forty of the latter per day hereafter. On August 18, 1884, one hundred freight cars were built in ten hours. The Allen Paper Car-wheel Company claims a capacity of fifteen thousand paper car-wheels a year. The brick-yards are large, and two hundred and twenty thousand bricks is one day's work. Many of the men who work in the brick-yards in summer harvest ice in winter, and it is expected to store about twenty-five thousand tons this winter. The carpenter shops, which do considerable work in Chicago, have employed at times as many as five hundred men. These are some of the principal material facts of interest to the general reader. Much could be said of Pullman as a manufacturing centre, but the purpose of this article is to treat it as an attempt to furnish laborers with the best homes under the most healthful conditions and with the most favorable surroundings in every respect, for Pullman aims to be a forerunner of better things for the laboring classes.

The questions to be answered are these: Is Pullman a success from a social standpoint? Is it worthy of imitation? Is it likely to inaugurate a new era in society? If only a partial success, what are its bright features and what its dark features?

THE STABLES.

Pullman as an attempt to realize an ideal must be judged by an ideal standard. The measure to be applied is the reasonable ideal of the social reformer. What is this ideal? Is it not that each individual be so situated as to participate, as fully as his nature will allow, in the advantages of the existing civilization? This is a high standard, but not so high as might at first appear. All those who have more than this measure calls for are by no means included in the class of *nouveaux riches*. The writer well remembers a visit to some brass-works in Balti-

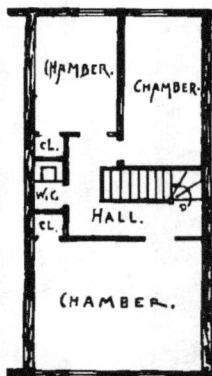

SECOND STORY.

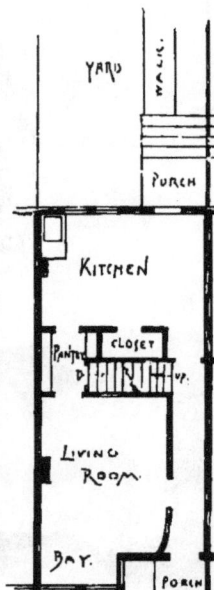

PLAN OF COTTAGES AT PULLMAN.

more, where rude, uneducated Welshmen were earning eighteen dollars a week. Society was doing well by these men, and in their case there could be no serious social question as far as wages were concerned. One needed to be with the men but a short time to be convinced that their income enabled them to participate in all the benefits of this nineteenth-century civilization which they were capable of enjoying. Now what the student of society wants to know is the nearness with which Pullman approaches the social ideal.

Very gratifying is the impression of the visitor who passes hurriedly through Pullman and observes only the splendid provision for the present material comforts of its residents. What is seen in a walk or drive through the streets is so pleasing to the eye that a woman's first exclamation is certain to be, "Perfectly lovely!" It is indeed a sight as rare as it

INTERIOR OF ARCADE—THE LIBRARY.

is delightful. What might have been taken for a wealthy suburban town is given up to busy workers, who literally earn their bread in the sweat of their brow. No favorable sites are set apart for drones living on past accumulations, and if a few short stretches are reserved for residences which can be rented only by those whose earnings are large, this is an exception; and it is not necessary to remain long in the place to notice that clergymen, officers of the company, and mechanics live in adjoining dwellings.

One of the most striking peculiarities of this place is the all-pervading air of thrift and providence. The most pleasing impression of general well-being is at once produced. Contrary to what is seen ordinarily in laborers' quarters, not a dilapidated door-step nor a broken window, stuffed perhaps with old clothing, is to be found in the city. The streets of Pullman, always kept in perfect condition, are wide and finely macadamized, and young shade trees on each side now ornament the town, and will in a few years afford refreshing protection from the rays of the summer sun.

Unity of design and an unexpected variety charm us as we saunter through the town. Lawns always of the same width separate the houses from the street, but they are so green and neatly trimmed that one can overlook this regularity of form. Although the houses are built in groups of two or more, and even in blocks, with

THE SCHOOL-HOUSE.

ingenious designs secure variety, of which the most skillful is probably the treatment of the sky line. Naturally, without an appearance of effort, it assumes an immense diversity. French roofs, square roofs, dormer-windows, turrets, sharp points, blunt points, triangles, irregular quadrangles, are devices resorted to in the upper stories to avoid the appearance of unbroken uniformity. A slight knowledge of mathematics shows how infinite the variety of possible combinations of a few elements, and a better appreciation of this fact than that exhibited by the architecture of Pullman it would be difficult to find. The streets cross each other at right angles, yet here again skill has avoided the frightful monotony of New York, which must sometimes tempt a nervous person to scream for relief. A public square, arcade, hotel, market, or some large building is often set across a street so ingeniously as to break the regular line, yet without inconvenience to traffic. Then at the termination of long streets a pleasing view greets and relieves the eye—a bit of water, a stretch of meadow, a clump of trees, or even one of the large but neat workshops. All this grows upon the visitor day by day. No other feature of Pullman can receive praise needing so little qualification as its architecture. Desirable houses have been provided for a large laboring population at so small a cost that they can be rented at rates within their

WORKING-MEN'S COTTAGES.

the exception of a few large buildings of cheap flats, they bear no resemblance to barracks; and one is not likely to make the mistake, so frequent in New York blocks of "brown-stone fronts," of getting into the wrong house by mistake. Simple but

means and yet yield a handsome return on the capital invested. Rents are probably about three-fifths what they are in Chicago, and, all things considered, this seems not to be an unfair standard of comparison. It is a mere matter of course that there are architectural defects even in Pullman. The diversity is not quite all that could be desired. What may be called the public buildings, that is to say, the hotel, school-house, arcade, etc., are detached, but no private house stands by itself, though there are quite a number of detached double houses. Spaces have, however, been reserved for a few detached private residences, which will improve the appearance of the town. With the exception of the church and parsonage, built of green serpentine stone from Philadelphia, all the buildings are of brick. This is monotonous, and rather wearying to the eye, but the slate roofs, and a large use of light stone trimmings, and stripes of black across the houses, help matters somewhat. The general character of the architecture is what has been called advanced secular Gothic. This is skillfully varied, and in the hotel particularly there is a feeling of the Queen Anne style. But there ought to be some bold break in the general design. The newness of things, which time will remedy, is a little distressing, as is also the mechanical regularity of the town, and it is this, perhaps, which suggests the epithet "machine-made." The growth of shade trees will break into the sameness, and the magnificent boulevard which divides the shops on the north from the residences on the south, stretching from east to west across the town, and bordered with double rows of elms, will, twenty years from now, be a vast improvement. Great overarching trees will hide one part of the town from another, and give opportunity for pleasant surprises in nature and art.

The interior of the houses affords scarcely less gratification than their exterior. Even the humblest suite of rooms in the flats is provided with water, gas, and closets, and no requisite of cleanliness is omitted. Most of the cottages are two stories in height, and contain five rooms, besides a cellar, closets, and pantry, as seen in the accompanying plan and illustrations. Quite a large number of houses contain seven rooms, and in these larger dwellings there is also a bath-room.

Outside of the home one finds other noteworthy provisions for the comfort, convenience, and well-being of the residents in Pullman. There is a large Market-house, 100 by 110 feet in size, through which a wide passage extends from east to west. This building contains a basement and two stories, the first divided into six-

teen stalls, the second a public hall. The dealers in meat and vegetables are concentrated in the Market-house. The finest building in Pullman is the Arcade, a structure 256 feet in length, 146 feet in width, and 90 feet in height. It is built of red pressed brick, with stone foundations and light stone trimmings, and a glass roof extends over the entire wide central passage. In the Arcade one finds offices, shops, the bank, theatre, library, etc. As no shops or stores are allowed in the town outside of the Arcade and Market-house, all shopping in Pullman is done under roof—a great convenience in wet weather, and a saving of time and strength.

The theatre, situated in the Arcade as just mentioned, seats eight hundred people, and is elegantly and tastefully furnished. The illustration on page 456 of the Arcade includes a view of the boxes, which are Moorish in design. It was intended to embrace in this theatre many of the best features of the Madison Square Theatre, but the scope of the present article does not admit of a detailed description of them, exquisite and perfectly appointed as they are. Representations are given by various troupes about once in two weeks. There is nothing peculiar in the management. The company rents it to applicants, but attempts to exclude immoral pieces, and admit only such as shall afford innocent amusement and instruction. The prices for tickets are thirty-five, fifty, and seventy-five cents, which have been found to be the most profitable in Pullman, higher prices keeping the people away, and lower ones not attracting enough more to compensate for the diminished return on each ticket.

In the interior of the Arcade a balcony extends around the passage in front of the rooms and offices of the second story, which it thus conveniently connects. It produces a pleasing effect, and affords a favorable position from which to view the busy throng below. The library, which opens on this balcony, contains six thousand volumes, the gift of Mr. Pullman, and numerous periodicals, among which were noticed several likely to be of special importance to mechanics, such as the *Railway Age*, the *Iron Age*, *Scientific American*, and *Popular Science Monthly*. The library rooms are elegantly furnished with Wilton carpets and plush-covered chairs, and the walls are beautifully painted. Objection has been raised to this luxuri-

ousness by those who think it re-
pels the ordinary artisan, unac-
customed in his own home to
such extravagance; but it must
be remembered that it is avowed-
ly part of the design of Pullman
to surround laborers as far as
possible with all the privileges of
large wealth. The annual charge
for the use of the Public Library,
for nothing in Pullman is free,
is three dollars—rather high for
workmen in these days of free libraries. The management of the
librarian is most commendable,
and every aid is given to those
who patronize it to render it as
instructive and elevating as possible. A special effort has been
made to induce the subscribers to
choose a superior class of litera-
ture, but the record shows that
seventy-five per centum of the
books drawn are still works of
fiction, which is about the usual
percentage in public libraries.

The educational facilities of
Pullman are those generally afforded in larger American villages by the public-school system.
The school trustees are elected by
the citizens, and rent of the Pullman Company a handsome building, which harmonizes in architecture and situation with the re-
mainder of the town.

There are no barns in the place,
but a large building provides ac-
commodation for livery-stables,
and a fire department sustained
by the Pullman Company. The
hotel, the property of the company, and managed by one of its
officers, is a large structure, surrounded on three sides by beautiful public squares covered with
flowers and shrubbery. It is
luxuriously furnished, admirably
kept, and contains the only bar-
room allowed in Pullman, though
there are thirty on the outskirts
of the place in Kensington. However, the temptation "to drink"
does not constantly stare one in
the face, and this restriction has
not entirely failed to accomplish
its end, the promotion of temper-
ance.

There is nothing so peculiar in

PLAN OF PULLMAN CITY.

these features of Pullman as to require further description. It was necessary to make brief mention of them to help the reader to understand the nature and extent of the experiment called Pullman.

The whole is the work of the Pullman Palace Car Company and the Pullman Land Association, which are both under one management, and, to a considerable extent, the same practically, although two separate legal persons. Colonel James Bowen, who appears to have been one of the interesting characters in the early history of Chicago, had long prophesied that the true site for a great city was upon the shores of Lake Calumet—an expanse of water some six feet deep, about three miles long, and a mile and a half wide, and connected with Lake Michigan by the Calumet River. Having found a believer in Mr. Pullman, he was commissioned by that gentleman to purchase quietly four thousand acres in the neighborhood, and this has become the site of Pullman. The entire town was built under the direction of a single architect, Mr. S. S. Beman, an ambitious young man whose frequently expressed desire for an opportunity to do a "big thing" was here gratified. This is probably the first time a single architect has ever constructed a whole town systematically upon scientific principles, and the success of the work entitles him to personal mention. The plans were drawn for a large city at the start, and these have been followed without break in the unity of design. Pullman illustrates and proves in many ways both the advantages of enterprises on a vast scale and the benefits of unified and intelligent municipal administration. All articles employed in the construction of the town were purchased at the lowest figures, as orders were given for unusually large quantities, and thus the outlay was far less than it would have been had each building, or even each block, been built by a separate individual. It is manifest, for example, that a man will obtain hinges at the most favorable rates who orders twenty-five thousand pairs at one time. An additional saving was effected by the establishment of the carpenter shops and brick-yards, which enabled the company to avoid the payment of profits on the wood-work and on the bricks. The bricks were manufactured of clay from the bottom of Lake Calumet, and thus the construction of the town helped to deepen its

harbor and prepare it for the large shipping which is one day expected there, for its proprietors prophesy that vessels will yet sail from Pullman to London. Then, as there is no competition at Pullman, and no conflicting municipal boards, gas, water, and sewerage pipes were laid once for all, and the pavement, when completed, not again disturbed. The money saved by this wise, unified, and consequently harmonious action must be reckoned by the hundred thousand.

There are over fifteen hundred buildings at Pullman, and the entire cost of the town, including all the manufacturing establishments, is estimated at eight millions of dollars. The rents of the dwellings vary from $4 50 per month for the cheapest flats of two rooms to $100 a month for the largest private house in the place. The rent usually paid varies from $14 to $25 a month, exclusive of the water charge, which is generally not far from eighty cents. A five-roomed cottage, such as is seen in the illustration, rents for $17 a month, and its cost is estimated at $1700, including a charge of $300 for the lot. But it must be understood that the estimated value of $1700 includes profits on brick and carpenter work and everything furnished by the company, for each industry at Pullman stands on its own feet, and keeps its own separate account. The company's brick-yards charge the company a profit on the brick the latter buys, and the other establishments do the same; consequently the estimated cost of the buildings includes profits which flowed after all into the company's coffers.

The Pullman companies retain everything. No private individual owns to-day a square rod of ground or a single structure in the entire town. No organization, not even a church, can occupy any other than rented quarters. With the exception of the management of the public school, every municipal act is here the act of a private corporation. What this means will be perceived when it is remembered that it includes such matters as the location, repairs, and cleaning of streets and sidewalks, the maintenance of the fire department, and the taking of the local census whenever desired. When the writer was in Pullman a census was taken. A superior officer of the company said to an inferior, "I want a census," and told what kind of a census was desired. That was the whole matter. The people of the place had no more to say about it than a resident of Kamtchatka. All this applies only to what is generally known as Pullman, which is in reality no political organization, and is called a town or city simply in a popular sense for the sake of convenience. Pullman is only a part of the large village and town of Hyde Park, but the latter appears to have relinquished the government of this portion of its territory bearing the name of Pullman to private corporations, and the writer was not able to find that a single resident of Pullman, not an officer of the Pullman companies, was either in the board of trustees of Hyde Park or in the staff of officers. The town clerk and treasurer are both officers of the Pullman Palace Car Company, and the directory of Hyde Park reveals the fact that with one exception every member of the board of education of the Pullman school district is an officer of the Palace Car Company or some concern which bears the name of Pullman.

One of Mr. Pullman's fundamental ideas is the *commercial value of beauty*, and this he has endeavored to carry out as faithfully in the town which bears his name as in the Pullman drawing-room and sleeping cars. He is one of the few men who have thought it a paying investment to expend millions for the purpose of surrounding laborers with objects of beauty and comfort. In a hundred ways one sees in Pullman to-day evidences of its founder's sagacious foresight. One of the most interesting is the fact that the company finds it pays them in dollars and cents to keep the streets sprinkled with water and the lawns well trimmed, the saving in paint and kalsomine more than repaying the outlay. Less dust and dirt are carried and blown into houses, and the injury done to walls and wood-work is diminished. For the rest, the neat exterior is a constant example, which is sure sooner or later to exert its proper effect on housewives, stimulating them to exertion in behalf of cleanliness and order.

It should be constantly borne in mind that all investments and outlays in Pullman are intended to yield financial returns satisfactory from a purely business point of view. The minimum return expected is six per centum on expenditure, and the town appears to have yielded a far higher percentage on cost up to the present time. Much of the land was bought at less than $200 per acre, and it is

likely that the average price paid did not exceed that. A large part of this now yields rent on a valuation of $5000 per acre, and certain sections in the heart of Pullman are to-day more valuable, and will continue to increase in value in the future, if the town grows as is expected. The extreme reluctance of the officers of the company to make precise statements of any kind renders it impossible to obtain the accurate information desired. Yet there seems to be no reason to doubt the emphatic assertion that the whole establishment pays handsomely. A large part of Pullman belongs to the Palace Car Company, which claims to have paid nine and one-half per centum on its entire stock for the last three years, and to have averaged about ten per centum since its organization in 1867. As far as the Land Association is concerned, it is sufficient to know that all its houses are rented at a high valuation, and the land put in at twenty-five times its cost.

It pays also in another way. The wholesome, cheerful surroundings enable the men to work more constantly and more efficiently. The healthy condition of the residents is a matter of general comment. The number of deaths has been about seven in a thousand per annum, whereas it has been about fifteen in a thousand in the rest of Hyde Park.

It is maintained that Pullman is truly a philanthropic undertaking, although it is intended that it should be a profitable investment, and this is the argument used: If it can be shown that it does pay to provide beautiful homes for laborers, accompanied with all the conditions requisite for wholesome living both for the body and the mind, the example set by Mr. Pullman will find wide imitation. If what is done for the residents of the town were simply a generous gift, another might argue, "If Mr. Pullman chooses to spend his money this way, very well! I have no objection, but I prefer to keep a stable of blooded horses. Each one according to his taste!" We may feel inclined to shrug our shoulders at the philanthropy which demands a good round sum for everything it offers, but certainly it is a great thing to have demonstrated the commercial value of beauty in a city of laborers.

The wages paid at Pullman are equal to those paid for similar services elsewhere in the vicinity. In a visit of ten days at Pullman no complaint was heard on this score which appeared to be well founded. Unskilled laborers—and they are perhaps one-fourth of the population —receive only $1 30 a day; but there are other corporations about Chicago which pay no more, and Pullman claims to pay only ordinary wages. Many of the mechanics earn $2 50 or $2 75 a day, some $3 and $4, and occasionally even more. Those who receive but $1 30 have a hard struggle to live, after the rent and water tax are paid. On this point there is unanimity of sentiment, and Pullman does comparatively little for them, and the social problem in their case remains unsolved. They are crowded together in the cheap flats, which are put as much out of sight as possible, and present a rather dreary appearance, although vastly better than the poorer class of New York tenements.

The great majority at Pullman are skilled artisans, and nearly all with whom the writer conversed expressed themselves as fairly well satisfied with their earnings, and many of them took pains to point out the advantages of the steady employment and prompt pay they always found there. The authorities even go out of their way to "make work" for one who has proved himself efficient and faithful.

There are many other pleasant and interesting features of Pullman, to which it is possible only to allude here. One is the perfect system of sewerage, similar to that which has been found so successful in Berlin, Germany. The sewerage is all collected in a great tank under the "water tower," and then pumped on to a large garden farm of one hundred and seventy acres, called the "Pullman Farm." This is already profitable, and it is hoped that in time it will pay interest on the cost of the entire sewerage system of the town, which was $300,000. It is worthy the careful study of municipal authorities.

There are a thousand and one little ways in which the residents of Pullman are benefited, and in many cases without cost to the company. Considerable care is taken to find suitable employment for those who in any way become incapacitated for their ordinary work. A watchman with a missing arm was seen, and a position as janitor was found for a man who had become partially paralyzed. These are but examples. Men temporarily injured receive full pay, save in cases

of gross carelessness, when one dollar a day is allowed. Employés are paid with checks on the "Pullman Loan and Savings Bank," to accustom them to its use and encourage them to make deposits.

Encouraging words from superiors are helpful. One warm-hearted official, to whom the welfare of the laboring classes appears to be a matter of momentous concern, wrote a note of thanks to the occupant of a cottage which was particularly well kept and ornamented with growing flowers. In another case he was so well pleased with the appearance of a cottage that he ordered a couple of plants in pots sent from the greenery to the lady of the house, with his compliments. The effect of systematic persistence in little acts of kind thoughtfulness like these is seen in the diffusion of a spirit of mutual helpfulness, and in frequent attempts to give practical, even if imperfect, expression to the truth of the brotherhood of man. Several ladies were especially prominent in this way, and among them may be mentioned the librarian. When the humbler young women see her home, which was designed for an ordinary mechanic, they often ask: "Can this be the same kind of a house we live in? Oh! how did you make all these pretty things? Please tell us." And a ready response is always given to their appeals. At a charming picnic, where a large number of residents were met, the writer had the pleasure of making the acquaintance of a great-hearted motherly German lady, the wife of a manager of the shops, whose life is spent in good works among the employés. The strangers are visited and brought into congenial social circles, and the poor and sick relieved in their distress, by this noble Christian woman. An interesting and successful experiment was tried in connection with wall-paper. Great quantities were bought at wholesale, and a man sent to the poorer houses with a number of varieties, from which the tenant was requested to select one, the company offering the paper at the very low figures at which they purchased it, and agreeing to hang it without charge. The architect assured the writer that this was doubtless the first time many women had been called upon to exercise taste and consider the beautiful in color in any matter pertaining to their dwellings. Great interest was aroused in the selection of wall-paper, and friends and neighbors were called in to aid in the discussion of colors and in the final choice. The small charge made was only beneficial; as it led the people to value what they had acquired.

These are the devices which, together with the constant example set by the company, have awakened a very general desire in the residents to adorn and beautify their dwellings. Everywhere, even in a flat of two rooms in the third story, one sees prints and engravings on the walls, Christmas and other cards, with cheap bric-à-brac on brackets in the corner, or on some inexpensive ornamental table, and growing plants in the windows. It is comparatively a small matter that a highly developed æstheticism could not approve of much that is seen, for it is only the beginning of an education of the higher faculties, and better things will be seen in the children.

. In the way of material comforts and beautiful surroundings, Pullman probably offers to the majority of its residents quite as much as they are in a position to enjoy, and in many cases even more. There are those who do not feel it a hardship to live in a dark alley of a great city, and there are men and women at Pullman incapable of appreciating its advantages. But they are learning to do it, and many who go away dissatisfied return, because they can not find elsewhere that to which they have become accustomed there. The pure air and perfect sanitary condition of the houses and of the entire city are more and more valued, especially by mothers, one of whom exclaimed to the writer, in speaking of Chicago: "I just hate the ugly old city." Pullman had taught her better things than she formerly knew, and thus it is becoming a great school, elevating laborers to a higher plane of wholesome living. The Commissioner of Health of Chicago, who holds that "healthy houses whose incumbency does not hint at the acceptance of charity are the best, in fact the only, means of teaching sanitation to the working classes," calls the emigrants from Pullman "sanitary missionaries."

But admirable as are the peculiarities of Pullman which have been described, certain unpleasant features of social life in that place are soon noticed by the careful observer, which moderate the enthusiasm one is at first inclined to feel upon an inspection of the external, plainly visible facts, and the picture must be completed before judgment can be pronounced upon it.

One just cause of complaint is what in government affairs would be called a bad civil service, that is, a bad administration in respect to the employment, retention, and promotion of employés. Change is constant in men and officers, and each new superior appears to have his own friends, whom he appoints to desirable positions. Favoritism and nepotism, out of place as they are in an ideal society, are oft-repeated and apparently well-substantiated charges.

. The resulting evil is very naturally dissatisfaction, a painful prevalence of petty jealousies, a discouragement of superior excellence, frequent change in the residents, and an all-pervading feeling of insecurity. Nobody regards Pullman as a real home, and, in fact, it can scarcely be said that there are more than temporary residents at Pullman. One woman told the writer she had been in Pullman two years, and that there were only three families among her acquaintances who were there when she came. Her reply to the question, "It is like living in a great hotel, is it not?" was, "We call it camping out." The nature of the leases aggravates this evil. As already stated, all the property in Pullman is owned by the Pullman associations, and every tenant holds his house on a lease which may be terminated on ten days' notice. A lease which lies on the table before the writer reads: "From —— to ——, unless sooner cancelled in accordance with the conditions of the lease." It is not necessary that any reason be assigned for the notice; "and it is expressly agreed that the fact that rent may have been paid at any time in advance shall not be a waiver of the right to put an end to the term and tenancy under this lease by such notice." Furthermore, three-fourths of the laborers in Pullman are employed by the Palace Car Company, and many of those who do not work for it are employed in establishments in which the company as such or a prominent member of it is interested. The power of Bismarck in Germany is utterly insignificant when compared with the power of the ruling authority of the Pullman Palace Car Company in Pullman. Whether the power be exercised rightfully or wrongfully, it is there all the same, and every man, woman, and child in the town is completely at its mercy, and it can be avoided only by emigration. It is impossible within the realm of Pullman to escape from the overshadowing influence of the company, and every resident feels this, and "monopoly" is a word which constantly falls on the ear of the visitor. Large as the place is, it supports no newspaper, through which complaints might find utterance, and one whose official position in the town qualified him to speak with knowledge declared positively that no publication would be allowed which was not under the direct influence of the Pullman Company. A Baptist clergyman, who had built up quite a congregation, once ventured to espouse the cause of a poor family ejected from their house, and gave rather public expression to his feelings. Shortly after his support began to fall away, one member after another leaving, and it has since never been possible to sustain a Baptist organization in Pullman. It is indeed a sad spectacle. Here is a population of eight thousand souls where not one single resident dare speak out openly his opinion about the town in which he lives. One feels that one is mingling with a dependent, servile people. There is an abundance of grievances, but if there lives in Pullman one man who would give expression to them in print over his own name, diligent inquiry continued for ten days was not sufficient to find him.

One gentleman, whose position ought to have exempted him from it, was "warned" in coming to Pullman to be careful in what he said openly about the town. It required recourse to some ingenuity to ascertain the real opinion of the people about their own city. While the writer does not feel at liberty to narrate his own experience, it can do no harm to mention a strange coincidence. While in the city the buttons on his wife's boots kept tearing off in the most remarkable manner, and it was necessary to try different shoemakers, and no one could avoid free discussion with a man who came on so harmless an errand as to have the buttons sewed on his wife's boots. This was only one of the devices employed. The men believe they are watched by the "company's spotter," and to let one of them know that information was desired about Pullman for publication was to close his lips to the honest expression of opinion. The women were inclined to be more outspoken.

An evil worthy of attention is the neglect of religion. There are scarcely accommodations for one-eighth of the population in the halls where religious exercises are conducted on Sunday. There is but one church building in Pullman. and that, the property of the company, is unoccupied because no denomination can pay the rent. The Presbyterians offered $2000 a year for it, and this was refused. The company, owning all the property of the place, does nothing for the support of religion. The Presbyterians receive $700 a year from the Presbyterian Board, and pay $600 of it over to the company for rent. The Methodists and Episcopalians also support small organizations with difficulty. The men say: "The company care nothing for our souls. They only want to get as much work as possible out of our bodies;" and forthwith they begin to neglect the provision others have made for their spiritual welfare. This may be illogical conduct, but it is human nature.

The town-meeting of New England has ever been regarded by writers of the highest authority on American government as one of the bulwarks of our liberties. The free discussion of local affairs, and the full responsibility for what is done and not done, have ever been held to be an education of the mind, a means to develop the qualities most useful in a citizen of a republic and a training for larger public duties. People of other countries are striving after a nearer approach to this in an improved local self-government, and the renowned German publicist Gneist is perhaps chiefly esteemed for what he has done to promote the movement in Germany. Yet in Pullman all this disappears. The citizen is surrounded by constant restraint and restriction, and everything is done for him, nothing by him.

The desire of the American to acquire a home is justly considered most commendable and hopeful. It promotes thrift and economy, and the habits acquired in the effort to pay for it are often the foundation of a future prosperous career. It is a beginning in the right direction. Again, a large number of house owners is a safeguard against violent movements of social discontent. Heretofore laborers at Pullman have not been allowed to acquire any real property in the place. There is a repression here as elsewhere of any marked individuality. Everything tends to stamp upon residents, as upon the town, the character expressed in "machine-made." Not only are strikes regarded as the chief of social sins, a view too widely disseminated by works like Charles Reade's *Put Yourself in His Place*, but individual initiative, even in affairs which concern the residents alone, is repressed. Once several of the men wanted to form a kind of mutual insurance association to insure themselves against loss of time in case of accident, but it was frowned down by the authorities, and nothing further has been heard of the matter. A lady attempted to found a permanent charitable organization to look after the poor and needy, but this likewise was discouraged, because it was feared that the impression might get abroad that there was pauperism in Pullman.

In looking over all the facts of the case the conclusion is unavoidable that the idea of Pullman is un-American. It is a nearer approach than anything the writer has seen to what appears to be the ideal of the great German Chancellor. It is not the American ideal. It is benevolent, well-wishing feudalism, which desires the happiness of the people, but in such way as shall please the authorities. One can not avoid thinking of the late Czar of Russia, Alexander II., to whom the welfare of his subjects was truly a matter of concern. He wanted them to be happy, but desired their happiness to proceed from him, in whom everything should centre. Serfs were freed, the knout abolished, and no insuperable objection raised to reforms, until his people showed a decided determination to take matters in their own hands, to govern themselves, and to seek their own happiness in their own way. Then he stopped the work of reform, and considered himself deeply aggrieved. The loss of authority and distrust of the people is the fatal weakness of many systems of reform and well-intentioned projects of benevolence.

Pullman ought to be appreciated, and high honor is due Mr. George M. Pullman. He has at least attempted to do something lasting and far-reaching, and the benefits he has actually conferred upon a laboring population of eight thousand souls testify that his heart must be warm toward his poorer brother. Mr. Pullman has partially solved one of the great problems of the immediate present, which is a diffusion of the benefits of concentrated wealth among wealth-creators.

Pullman is still in its infancy, and great things are promised in the future. On an adjoining tract lots are now offered for sale, and workmen will be aided in the purchase of these, and encouraged to build houses thereon. Other manufacturing establishments are expected soon, and a more extended and diversified industry will render the laborers less dependent. Mr. Pullman has also at heart numerous plans, the purpose of which is to give employment to women and young people. It is further proposed to establish a manual training school, and the inevitable Western university is talked about. It is to be hoped that what has been begun at Pullman will be continued in a larger spirit, and that a grander structure will arise on foundations already laid. It is especially to be desired that means should be discovered to awaken in the residents an interest and a pride in Pullman. It is now thought a praiseworthy thing "to beat the company," which phrase in itself points to something radically wrong. It is quite practicable to develop a democracy, or at least what might be called a constitutional monarchy, out of the despotism of Pullman. It is not more than has been done elsewhere, as, for example, by M. Godin, at Guise, France, where the affairs of the "Social Palace" are managed by committees of laborers elected by laborers. Some co-operative features might be added, which would be a move in the right direction, and every great philanthropic enterprise ought as soon as possible to be placed on such a footing as not to be dependent upon the life of any one individual. Not a few have ventured to express the hope that Pullman might be widely imitated, and thus inaugurate a new era in the history of labor. But if this signifies approval of a scheme which would immesh our laborers in a net-work of communities owned and managed by industrial superiors, then let every patriotic American cry, God forbid! What would this mean? The establishment of the most absolute power of capital, and the repression of all freedom. It matters not that they are well-meaning capitalists; all capitalists are not devoted heart and soul to the interests of their employés, and the history of the world has long ago demonstrated that no class of men are fit to be intrusted with unlimited power. In the hour of temptation and pressure it is abused, and the real nature of the abuse may for a time be concealed even from him guilty of it; but it degrades the dependent, corrupts the morals of the superior, and finally that is done unblushingly in the light which was once scarcely allowed in a dark corner. .This is the history of a large share of the degeneracy of manners and morals in public and private life.

No; the body is more than raiment, and the soul more than the body. If free American institutions are to be preserved, we want no race of men reared as underlings and with the spirit of menials. John Stuart Mill and others have regarded the relation of master and servant, employer and employed, as unworthy of the highest attainable average type of manhood and womanhood, and have prophesied the abolition of such relationship, and the establishment of some kind or another of co-operation, where men will work for and with one another. Perhaps that may seem Utopian, but it is possible to strive for it as an ideal, and it is the goal toward which the wisest philanthropists are pushing. Shall we turn about and forge new bonds of dependence? Is not a tendency to do this observable as

one of the signs of the time? Are we not frequently trying to offer the gilded cage as a substitute for personal liberty? When John Most, in an address to the laborers of Baltimore, sneered at this much-vaunted American liberty, and asked, "Of what value is it? Has any one ever been able to clothe himself with it, to house himself in it, or to satisfy with it the cravings of his stomach?" did he not give a gross expression to a kind of materialism which is becoming too common? It is idle to deny the spread of luxury, and numerous defalcations and embezzlements bear witness to wide-extended extravagance, an overvaluation of material comforts, and an undervaluation of the higher ethical goods. So when we see such splendid provision for the body as at Pullman, we clap our hands and stop not to ask how all this is to effect the formation of character. And the impassioned pleas for liberty which moved Americans mightily one hundred years ago fall to-day on the ear as something strange and ridiculous. Such thing are straws floating on the stream of social life. Have we reason to be pleased with the direction in which the current is setting?

EAST ANGELS.

CHAPTER II.

THE Doctor admitted that Garda could converse in Spanish. He suggested that they should walk on and join her. Joining her, of course, meant joining De Torrez. The Cuban proved to be a dark-skinned youth, with dull black eyes, a thin face, and black hair, closely cut, that stood up in straight short thickness all over his head, defying a parting. He was tall, gaunt, with a great want of breadth in the long expanse of his person; he was deliberate in his motions, ungainly. Yet he could not have been described as insignificant exactly, because of a certain deep reticent consciousness of his own importance, which was visible in every one of his slow, stiff movements, in every glance of his dull, reserved eyes. He bowed profoundly when introduced to the Northerner; but said nothing. He did not speak after the others came up. When Garda addressed him, he contented himself with another bow.

They all walked on together, and after some minutes the little ridge, winding with its sentinel bayonets across old fields, brought them to the main avenue of the place. This old road, broad as it was, was completely overarched by the great live-oaks which bordered it on each side. Their boughs rose high in the air, met, interlaced, and passed on, each stretching completely over the centre of the road-way, and curving downward on the opposite side; looking east and looking west was like looking through a Gothic aisle, vaulted in gray-green. The little party entered this avenue.. Garda, after a few moments, again separated herself from Winthrop and Dr. Kirby, and walked on in advance with De Torrez. The Doctor looked after them, discomfited.

"We should have spoken Spanish," said Winthrop, smiling.

"I do not know a word of the language," declared the Doctor, with something of the frankness of fatigue in his voice.

For the Doctor was not in the habit of

www.ingramcontent.com/pod-product-compliance
Lightning Source LLC
Chambersburg PA
CBHW021622290326
41931CB00047B/1438